WITHDRAWN

Rosie's **R** Book

WRITTEN BY **J. L. MAZZEO**
ILLUSTRATED BY **HELEN ROSS REVUTSKY**

dingles & company New Jersey

First Printing

Published By dingles&company
P.O. Box 508
Sea Girt, New Jersey 08750

LIBRARY OF CONGRESS CATALOG CARD NUMBER
2005907287

ISBN
ISBN-13: 978 1-59646-518-3
ISBN-10: 1-59646-518-2

Printed in the United States of America

My Letter Library series is based on the original concept of Judy Mazzeo Zocchi.

ART DIRECTION
Barbie Lambert & Rizco Design
DESIGN
Rizco Design
EDITED BY
Andrea Curley
PROJECT MANAGER
Lisa Aldorasi
EDUCATIONAL CONSULTANT
Maura Ruane McKenna
PRE-PRESS BY
Pixel Graphics

EXPLORE THE LETTERS OF THE ALPHABET WITH MY LETTER LIBRARY*

Aimee's **A** Book
Bebe's **B** Book
Cassie's **C** Book
Delia's **D** Book
Emma's **E** Book
Faye's **F** Book
George's **G** Book
Henry's **H** Book
Izzy's **I** Book
Jade's **J** Book
Kelsey's **K** Book
Logan's **L** Book
Mia's **M** Book
Nate's **N** Book
Owen's **O** Book
Peter's **P** Book
Quinn's **Q** Book
Rosie's **R** Book
Sofie's **S** Book
Tad's **T** Book
Uri's **U** Book
Vera's **V** Book
Will's **W** Book
Xavia's **X** Book
Yola's **Y** Book
Zach's **Z** Book

* All titles also available in bilingual English/Spanish versions.

WEBSITE
www.dingles.com
E-MAIL
info@dingles.com

J
P
MAZZEO
6/18 5.85

Rr

My Letter Library leads young children through the alphabet one letter at a time. By focusing on an individual letter in each book, the series allows youngsters to identify and absorb the concept of each letter thoroughly before being introduced to the next. In addition, it invites them to look around and discover where objects beginning with the specific letter appear in their own world.

Aa Bb Cc Dd Ee Ff Gg

Hh Ii Jj Kk Ll Mm Nn

Oo Pp Qq **Rr** Ss Tt Uu

Vv Ww Xx Yy Zz

R is for **R**osie.

Rosie is a **r**esponsible **r**abbit.

In Rosie's bathroom

you will see a **r**uby **r**ing,

R r

a **r**ibbon made of silk,

R r

and a soft rug
to stand on.

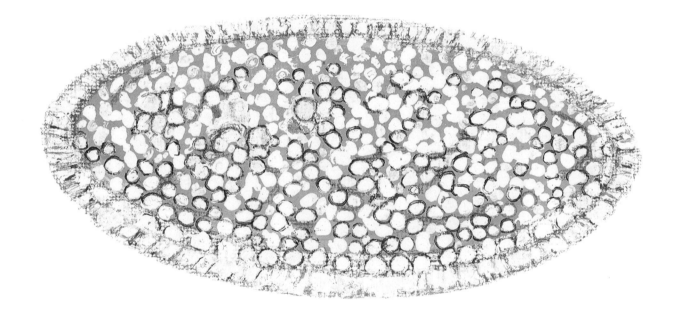

R r

While in Rosie's bathtub
you can shake a toy rattle,

Rr

splash with

a yellow **r**ubber duck,

R r

or play with

a squeaky toy rat.

Rr

When you look

around Rosie's bathroom

you will find

three pretty **r**osebuds,

R r

a bottle of her mother's
rosewater,

ROSEWATER

R r

and a **r**adio

that plays music.

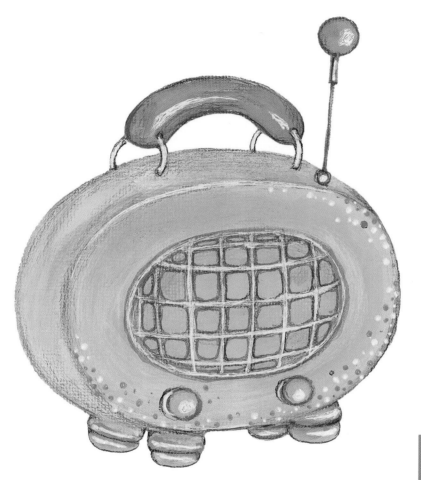

Rr

Things that begin with the letter **R** are all around.

RUBY **R**ING

RIBBON

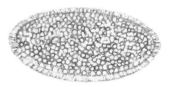

RUG

RATTLE

RUBBER DUCK

RAT

ROSEBUDS

BOTTLE OF **R**OSEWATER

RADIO

Where in Rosie's bathroom can they be found?

Have an **"R"** Day!

Read "R" stories all day long.
Read books about rubies, rugs, and other **R** words. Then have the child pick out all of the words and pictures starting with the letter **R.**

Make an "R" Craft: Rainbow Art
Follow this acronym, ROY G BIV, to help the child learn the order of the colors in a rainbow.

Have the child dip a paintbrush or a small sponge in red paint.

Then have the child paint a large red arc on a large piece of white construction paper with the paintbrush or sponge. Rinse the paintbrush or sponge thoroughly.

Have the child repeat the previous steps with each color of the rainbow. (Remember, the letters in the acronym represent the colors in a rainbow and the order they follow: red, orange, yellow, green, blue, indigo, and violet.)

Not only will the child learn the colors of the rainbow, he or she will have a beautiful Rainbow Art wall hanging!

Make an "R" Snack: Raspberry Roll Ups
- Open a package of crescent roll dough and preheat the oven as indicated on the package.
- Unroll the dough and gently pull apart the precut pieces of dough.
- Lay the pieces on a cookie sheet.
- Have the child spread a thin layer of raspberry jam on each piece of dough with a plastic knife.
- Starting from the widest side, let the child roll the dough to the tip of the triangle.
- Bake the Raspberry Roll Ups according to the directions on the package.
- Let them cool, and enjoy!

For additional **"R"** Day ideas and a reading list, go to www.dingles.com.

About **Letters**

Use the My Letter Library series to teach a child to identify letters and recognize the sounds they make by hearing them used and repeated in each story.

Ask:
- What letter is this book about?
- Can you name all of the **R** pictures on each page?
- Which **R** picture is your favorite? Why?
- Can you find all of the words in this book that begin with the letter **R**?

ENVIRONMENT
Discuss objects that begin with the letter **R** in the child's immediate surroundings and environment.

Use these questions to further the conversation:
- What is your bathroom like?
- Do you share the bathroom with anyone? If so, with whom?
- Do you have a stuffed or real rabbit? If so, what is his or her name?
- Do you have a favorite food that starts with the letter **R**? What is It?

OBSERVATIONS
The My Letter Library series can be used to enhance the child's imagination. Encourage the child to look around and tell you what he or she sees.

Ask:
- Do you have a radio in your house? Do you sing and dance to the music?
- Do you have a rubber duck in your bathtub? If not, what do you play with when you take a bath?
- What is your favorite **R** object at home? Why?
- Do you know where a rainbow comes from? Which is your favorite color in a rainbow?

TRY SOMETHING NEW...
Ask a parent to help you look up information about rainbows. Try to find out how they are formed, what colors are involved, and what some people believe you can find at the end of one!

J. L. MAZZEO grew up in Middletown, New Jersey, as part of a close-knit Italian American family. She currently resides in Monmouth County, New Jersey, and still remains close to family members in heart and home.

HELEN ROSS REVUTSKY was born in St. Petersburg, Russia, where she received a degree in stage artistry/design. She worked as the directing artist in Kiev's famous Governmental Puppet Theatre. Her first book, *I Can Read the Alphabet,* was published in Moscow in 1998. Helen now lives in London, where she has illustrated several children's books.